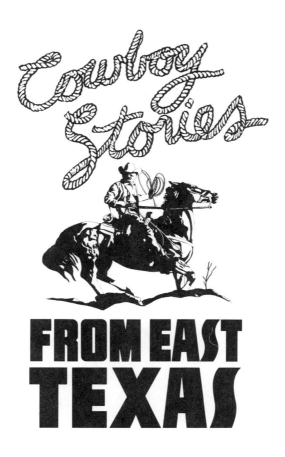

Cowboy Stories FROM EAST TEXAS

by John Lash

Illustrations by John Lash

Hendrick-Long Publishing Co.

Dallas

Dedication

This book is dedicated to the children of Texas,
especially Daddy Bob's and Nanny's grandchildren:
Lukas Lash, Sambo Lash, Magdalena Lash, Macon Lash,
Christy Lash, Jessica Lash, Joe Cody Lash,
and Bonnie Morris

Library of Congress Cataloging-in-Publication Data

Lash, John, date
    Cowboy stories from east Texas / by John Lash; illustrations by John
Lash.
        p.   cm.
        Contents: Introduction—Bubba and the bad cow—Ears and the
rodeo—Lep and the wild hog—Uncle Marshall and the longhorn bull—The
hurricane calf—Toby Frederick's three goats—Bubba and Snake—Daddy Bob
and Moses, the alligator.
        ISBN 0-937460-66-4   ISBN 1-885777-27-2 (sc)
        [1. Cowboys—Fiction. 2. Texas—Fiction.] I. Title.
PZ7.L32718Co 1991
[Fic]—dc20   90-28880
                                                                CIP
                                                                 AC

Design and Production:
Flying Colors Studio

Hendrick-Long Publishing Co.
Dallas, Texas 75225

Contents

Introduction

The stories in this book are about Daddy Bob, the best cowboy who ever came out of Texas. Now, people who have never been there think that Texas is only dirt, rock, and cactus. West Texas is a lot like that, but Texas is a very big place, and the land is not the same everywhere. Central Texas is a place of rolling hills, clear blue rivers, and miles and miles of beautiful wildflowers. The bluebonnet is the Texas state flower, and when it blooms, the land is bright blue as far as the eye can see.

South Texas is as flat as a table, with vast plains of grass, palm trees, and sparkling white beaches along the Gulf of Mexico. But east Texas, and that is where Daddy Bob lives, is forests, swamps, bayous, and dark muddy rivers flowing to the Gulf. East Texas is sometimes called The Big Thicket because the forests go for hundreds of miles through Texas, Louisiana, and Arkansas. The trees and brush grow so thick together that a man has trouble walking, and there are many places where the sun never touches the ground.

Most of the forests are made up of pine trees, and that is why many people call east Texas the Piney Woods. Of course, there are many other kinds of trees there. There are huge cypress trees that grow in the swamps right out of the water, dogwoods with pink crosses on their white flowers, ironwood tress too hard to cut, crab apple trees, oak trees, huckleberry trees, and many others. Filling the space between the trees are honeysuckle vines with little yellow and white flowers that the children pick so they can suck the honey out. There are lots of blackberry and mayhaw bushes. In the summer, children pick blackberries and mayhaws and sell them to women who want to make jelly.

Sometimes when you walk or ride your horse through the east Texas forests, you can see saw grass marshes. A saw grass marsh looks like a field of grass, but if you go into it, you will find that the ground is muddy and soft and that some of the grass is on tiny islands that are floating on top of the water. Often there is quicksand, and if a man or an animal steps in it, he can sink completely out of sight.

Many people still live on ranches or farms in east Texas. A place is a farm if it raises crops and if the cows are taken care of by men on foot. It is a ranch if it has cows that are taken care of by men on horses. These men are the cowboys. Of course, some of the people live in small towns and are called "townies." They are mostly storekeepers, doctors, schoolteachers, barbers, and other townie things.

In east Texas, the forests can be so dark and spooky at night, with mists and strange noises, that it might just seem natural to believe in ghosts and spirits, as some people do. Some east Texas towns even have a haunted house that the local children try to sneak into at night so they can look for a ghost. The forests are full of unseen creatures, like the "wampus cat," which is supposed to be part panther and part man. People say that at night you can hear its screams and that it sounds just like a woman screaming for help. Sometimes hunters and fishermen disappear in the Big Thicket, never to be seen again. They will hear what they think is a woman screaming and they will go to find her and never come back. People say that the wampus cat got them. So, if you are ever in east Texas in the forest at night and you hear screaming, just get a little closer to the fire, and do not let anyone go off alone.

But there are not just ghosts and monsters that inhabit the forests. There are many kinds of animals, some of which are very dangerous. The cows in east Texas are wild and learn to fight very young so that they can protect themselves against the other animals of the forest. When they see a cowboy coming on his horse, they are ready to fight him just as they would any other animal. Some cows are so ready to fight that they will come hunting a man if they smell him.

There are also wild hogs called "piney-wood rooters" that have tusks for cutting and sticking their enemies. No one wants to have trouble with a wild hog. Usually they will run away when they see a man coming, but if they cannot run away, they go crazy and are ready to fight anything.

In the autumn, black panthers will come south from the Davy Crockett National Forest on their way to the warmer weather along the Louisiana-Texas border. When the panthers pass the farms and ranches, the cows get nervous. If the winter becomes very cold, wolves will sometimes make the same journey.

The east Texas forests also have poisonous snakes and spiders. The coral snake is a pretty snake with its red, yellow, and black rings, and it is also the most poisonous. If a cowboy gets bitten by a coral snake, he does not have much chance of surviving. Luckily, the coral snake does not have fangs but only rows of tiny teeth in a very small mouth. The coral snake cannot bite you very easily because it cannot open its mouth very wide. It has to bite you in a small place, like the earlobe or the skin between your fingers.

Though not so poisonous, the cottonmouth is a much more dangerous snake. It can swim, and on land, it can jump forward. If it is angry, it will chase you. It usually stays around rivers and swamps, or any place where there is water.

The copperhead snake has a red mark on the top of its

head. You have to be careful when walking in the forest and remember not to step over logs, because copperheads like to lie under logs in the shade and will bite your foot. East Texans usually know to step on top of a log and jump out away from it to come down.

There are also a few rattlesnakes in the forests, but they usually do not get as big as the ones in west Texas. Rattlesnakes are easier to avoid than the copperheads because they warn you that you are getting too close by rattling their tails.

Sometimes you can see big black hairy spiders called tarantulas in east Texas. There are not many because they like dry places, and in east Texas there is always a lot of rain. If a tarantula bites you, it only makes you sick. A much more dangerous spider is the black widow. It is very small and shiny-black with a red hourglass figure on its stomach. The black widow likes to live in piles of brush and wood stacks, so east Texans wear gloves when they have to work picking up fence posts or old boards.

There are alligators in the rivers, swamps, and bayous that the cowboys have to watch for when they are driving their cows through the water. The alligators share the rivers and bayous with the snapping turtles that can snap a finger off, and giant catfish, five or six feet long, that can eat a dog or other small animal. No one is really sure how big those catfish can grow. One time there was a man working at Dam B, the dam between Woodville and Jasper.

This man had to dive into the dark murky water to work on the gate that lets the water out of the dam. After working for a few minutes, he felt something bump against his back. He turned around and saw two eyes about two feet apart. It was a giant catfish as big as a horse. He got out of the water as fast as he could and told everyone that he would never go down there again.

Of course, there are many other animals in the east Texas forests that are not so dangerous. East Texas has deer, raccoons, opossums, ducks, pelicans, bats, doves, wild horses, crawfish, cranes, herons, hawks, skunks, wildcats, porcupines, armadillos, rabbits, squirrels, muskrats, and many others.

It was here in these vast piney woods that Daddy Bob lived with his wife, Nanny, and their little boy, Bubba. Their ranch was on a small hill in a forest clearing about seven miles from the little town of Mauriceville. Daddy Bob had about two hundred cows in the forest, some wild hogs that he had marked on the ears so that everyone would know they belonged to him, a few goats, turkeys, geese, ducks, and chickens. Daddy Bob and his family were poor, but they were happy living with their animals and the forest all around them.

Bubba and the Bad Cow

When Daddy Bob's little boy, Bubba, was six years old, he had to start school. It was not easy for him to get to the school because Daddy Bob lived seven miles from town. Bubba had to walk three miles down a dirt road through the forest before he came to the farm road where the school bus would pick him up.

Bubba was excited about beginning school. The first day he got up early, dressed, and went out to the chicken house. It was his job to take care of the chickens. He let the chickens out of the chicken house so that they could wander around the whole ranch. Then he sprinkled a little chicken feed around the yard for them. The turkeys and guineas came down out of the trees, the geese came from under the house, and the ducks came waddling up from the pond, all trying to get a share of the feed before the chickens could eat it all.

As he was going back into the house, Bubba saw Daddy Bob out in the barn feeding the horses. Nanny was waiting for him in the kitchen with a big plate of hot cakes and maple syrup. After breakfast, Bubba put on his school bag, kissed Nanny and Daddy Bob goodbye, and started walking down the dirt road through the forest.

As he crossed the old wooden bridge on Cow Bayou, Bubba saw a raccoon hanging onto a pine tree and looking at him. He wanted to stop and play with it a little, but he knew he must not be late for the bus. Nanny would be mad if he missed his ride. He saw a herd of five deer at the edge of Elbow Marsh. He stopped to watch them eat for a few minutes, then hurried on. Just before getting to the farm road, he saw a set of tracks crossing the dirt road and going off toward Uncle Marshall's place. He bent down to look at them and saw that they were wild hog tracks. He heard the school bus coming and had to run the rest of the way to the road so he would not miss it.

The bus brought Bubba back to the dirt road when school was out that afternoon. As the bus left, he waved goodbye to the other children and began walking home. Near Elbow Marsh, he heard something moving in the forest. Through the trees he could see some brown hair. Then the brush along the road behind him opened, and out stepped an old brindle-colored Longhorn cow. She was looking at him and pawing the dirt with her hoofs. He could see that she was preparing to charge him.

Bubba threw down his school bag and started running as fast as he could down the road. He knew he could not outrun the cow, so he ran to a pine tree growing by the side of the road and started climbing. He got pine sap all over his hands and clothes, and he tore his shirt on a broken limb, but he managed to climb to a limb big enough to hold him.

The cow charged up to the tree and started pawing the ground again. She was looking up the tree at him, shaking her horns and bellowing. Bubba was scared, but he knew that the cow could not reach him where he was sitting in the tree.

After a while the cow got tired of just standing there and began eating the grass at the foot of the tree. As she ate, she began to wander away. Bubba waited until he thought she was far enough away and then very slowly began to climb down. When he got to the ground, he tiptoed toward the road. He was about ten feet from the tree when the cow jerked her head up and saw him. She lowered her horns and charged at him. Bubba turned around and raced back to the tree. The cow was right on him and caught one of his pants legs with her horn as he was climbing up. Bubba jerked his leg up and the horn tore a big hole in his pants.

The cow just stood there looking up at him. Bubba picked some pine cones off the branches nearest him and began throwing them at her. One hit her right between the eyes. Boy, that cow was angry! After a while, she began to eat again. She wandered away from the tree, but Bubba was not going to come down that tree again. He was afraid she would get him the next time.

Bubba sat in the tree for about an hour wishing that someone would come along to help him, or that the cow would go away. He was tired, thirsty, and hungry. He was about to start crying when he heard something. It was a dog barking, and the sound was getting closer. Bubba said, "I know that bark! That's Rock, our cowdog!" Then he heard a horse running. Bubba stood up on the limb and saw Daddy Bob riding on his best cowhorse, Tom, with Rock running beside him. Bubba yelled, "Daddy Bob! Daddy Bob!"

The brindle cow looked up and saw Daddy Bob coming after her. She spun around to run for the forest, but before she could start to run, Rock bit her on the back leg. Daddy Bob was waving an eight-foot-long bullwhip over his head and popping it. *Pow! Pow! Pow!* Well, that cow took off and started running as fast as she could for the deep woods, but Daddy Bob was right behind her. Rock was barking and biting her heels, Tom was biting her on the rear end, and Daddy Bob was laying that bullwhip right down the middle of her back. *Pow! Pow!* Bubba saw them all disappear into the woods, but he could still hear the whip popping, Rock barking, and the cow bellowing.

Bubba climbed down from the tree, and in a little while Rock came running out of the forest with Daddy Bob and Tom right behind him. Daddy Bob said, "Well, that is one cow that knows not to chase Daddy Bob's little boy." He helped Bubba into the saddle and they rode home.

When they got there, Nanny wanted to know what had happened. Daddy Bob said, "Bubba was chased up a tree by that old brindle cow."

The next morning, Daddy Bob loaded a pile of boards and fence posts into the back of his pickup truck along with a hammer, nails, and a post-hole digger. He told Bubba,

"You get your pony out of the barn and put your saddle on him." Bubba saddled his pony, Flag, and instead of walking down the road to the school bus, he rode Flag. When the school bus came, he tied Flag to a tree and went to school.

Daddy Bob drove his pickup truck to the bus stop and unloaded the boards and posts. He took the post-hole digger and dug holes for all the posts, put the posts in, and nailed the boards to them so that he had a small but strong corral with a big oak tree in it for shade. Then Daddy Bob went back to the pickup and got a big washtub, put it in the corral, and filled it with water from the creek. He untied Flag, took the saddle and bridle off, and put him in the corral.

When Bubba got off the bus that afternoon, he saw Flag in the little corral. He saddled him up and rode home. He did not have to worry about the brindle cow now because he knew Flag could outrun her. From then on, every school morning, Bubba would saddle Flag and ride to the road. He would leave Flag in the corral and go to school. In the afternoon, after school, he would get Flag and ride him home.

Ears and the Rodeo

Daddy Bob had a Brahma bull called Ears. This bull weighed about three thousand pounds and had a big hump on his back. He was gray-colored and had two long floppy ears hanging all the way down past his jaw. Those long ears were how he got his name. He was the biggest, meanest bull in Texas.

Anyone who knows about Brahma bulls knows that they are naturally mean. East Texans have Brahmas because it takes a strong, tough bull to stay alive in the forest and to protect the cows from wild animals. Ears grew up in the forest fighting wolves, alligators, panthers, snakes, and vultures. All the wild animals knew to leave Ears and his cows alone.

Sometimes bulls that belonged to another cowboy would come to Ears's part of the forest and try to take his cows away from him. In the spring you could hear the bulls fighting, but none of them ever beat Ears.

Mauriceville is a small town with about one hundred people, so there is not much entertainment that the people do not make for themselves. There are no movie theaters, golf courses, or football games. But once a year, on a warm summer day, Mauriceville has a rodeo. The town has a rodeo arena, and cowboys come from miles around with their families to see who the best riders and ropers are. They rope calves, wrestle steers, ride wild horses and bulls, and race around barrels.

One summer it was time for the rodeo, and all the cowboys were trying to finish their work early so that they could go. "Wild Bill" Meeks was the man who had to bring the bucking horses, bulls, and other animals to the rodeo. He was from Vidor, which was only about twenty miles from Mauriceville. The morning of the rodeo he was out loading his animals in the truck to take them to Mauriceville when he saw that his best bucking bull was sick. He knew he would have to find another bull very quickly because the rodeo was that afternoon.

Wild Bill drove his big truck to Mauriceville and stopped at the feed store. He went in and asked the storekeeper, "Do you know anyone around here that has a bull that will buck?"

The storekeeper said, "Daddy Bob has a bull out at his ranch that is the biggest, meanest bull I have ever seen. I just know his bull will buck!"

Wild Bill thanked the storekeeper, got in his truck, and drove out to Daddy Bob's place. He saw Daddy Bob and Bubba cleaning their saddles in front of the barn. He got out of the truck and went over to them.

Daddy Bob said, "Howdy! Can I help you?"

Wild Bill answered, "Howdy, Daddy Bob! My name is Wild Bill Meeks." Then he told him about his sick bull. "I really need another bull," Wild Bill said. "I heard you have a bull that might be good in the rodeo. I'll give you twenty dollars if you'll lend him to me."

Daddy Bob agreed and told Bubba to go into the house and telephone Danny Barrow to come over and help him catch Ears. Then he began to saddle Tom and Flag.

In about half an hour, Danny Barrow's pickup truck and horse trailer came rolling into the yard. Danny Barrow was the horseshoer. He was going to wrestle steers at the rodeo, and he was one of the best cowboys anywhere. Wild Bill stayed with his truck while Daddy Bob, Danny Barrow, and Bubba rode off into the forest with their cowdogs Rock, Brindle, and Lep running ahead sniffing the ground for signs of Ears. Daddy Bob always had good cowdogs because it was almost impossible to find cows in the forest without them.

Daddy Bob said to Danny, "The last time I saw Ears he was down in Elbow Marsh, so let's head that way."

When they got to the edge of the marsh, Rock started barking and all the dogs took off running. Daddy Bob saw Ears come charging out from a blackberry thicket followed by three or four cows. Daddy Bob and Danny untied their ropes and made lassos while they spurred their horses after Ears.

Ears was running, trying to get into the deep woods. He knew that if he could get in there, it would be hard for the cowboys to throw their ropes because the trees were so close together. But before he could make it, Rock jumped up and caught Ears on the nose. Lep and Brindle came to help Rock, and they turned Ears toward a big clearing. Now Ears was in the open. Daddy Bob raced Tom around Ears's left side and threw his lasso right over Ears's horns. Danny came riding up on the right side, and before Ears could turn to attack Daddy Bob and Tom, Danny caught Ears with his own lasso.

Now Ears was caught between Daddy Bob and Danny, and the horses kept the ropes tight so that Ears could not turn either way. Together Daddy Bob and Danny led Ears out of the forest while Bubba blew his cow horn to call the dogs away. When they got back to the house, they loaded Ears into Wild Bill's truck. Wild Bill thanked Daddy Bob, gave him the twenty dollars, and drove away to the rodeo grounds.

That afternoon, Daddy Bob and Bubba loaded Tom and

Flag into the horse trailer, got into the pickup truck with Nanny, and drove to Mauriceville. They drove into the rodeo grounds and unloaded the horses. Daddy Bob belonged to the Orange, Texas, Sheriff's Posse and was supposed to carry the Texas flag in the Grand Entry parade when all the cowboys would ride around the rodeo arena. Nanny went up into the stands and sat with Danny Barrow's wife and little girls.

The Grand Entry began, and the Sheriff's Posse came riding in led by Daddy Bob carrying the Texas flag. All the cowboys and cowgirls followed, with little Bubba and Flag at the end of the line, while the rodeo band played "The Yellow Rose of Texas."

After the Grand Entry, Daddy Bob rode back into the arena. He was one of the pick-up men. The pick-up men had to help the cowboys get off the bucking horses when the whistle blew to end the ride, and they were supposed to keep the bulls from hurting cowboys who had bucked off.

The rodeo started with the bareback bronc riding. In bareback the cowboy must ride a bucking horse with no saddle. Frank DuBois from the town of Spurger won the bareback championship.

Next came the saddle-bronc riding and then the steer wrestling. In steer wrestling, the cowboy must jump from his running horse onto a steer, grab its horns, and throw it to the ground. Nanny, Daddy Bob, and Bubba cheered and cheered when Danny Barrow won. Later everyone was even happier when Daddy Bob won the calf roping.

Finally it was time for the bull riding. Everyone was sure Slim Windham from Silsbee would win because he was the best bull rider in east Texas. When the bulls were in the bucking chutes, the first cowboy bucked out. The bulls bucked and churned up the dirt with the cowboys yelling and the bulls bellowing. Well, some cowboys got thrown and some bulls got ridden. Slim Windham made a great ride on a big Hereford bull, and everyone knew that he was winning.

There was only one cowboy left to ride, Bucky Richards. Bucky was from Kirbyville and worked for the Muckleroy Cattle Company. He was a good cowboy, and if anyone could beat Slim Windham it would be Bucky.

Ears was the only bull left, and they put him in the bucking chute. Bucky climbed up on the chute, put his bull rope on, and sat down on Ears's back. He held his hand up and said, "Open the gate!" Well, they opened the gate, and my goodness! That bull of Daddy Bob's came out of the chute like a tornado. Ears threw Bucky clear over the chute gate. Bucky did not even ride for a second.

The people in the stands were quiet. They could not believe how Ears had thrown Bucky in the dirt so easily. Another good bull rider named Henry Joe Spurlock said that he wanted to try to ride Ears. All the people cheered. So they put Ears back in the chute. Henry Joe got on, pulled his cowboy hat down tight, and said, "No bull is

going to throw me like that!" Then he yelled, "Open the gate!" Out of the chute Ears came, and Lord have mercy! Ears was in the air turning a circle, and when he came down, the dirt flew all the way up into the stands. Then Ears started spinning around and bucking at the same time. Henry Joe just could not hang on any longer and went flying through the air. *Slam!* He landed on his face and had dirt all in his nose, his ears, and his mouth. Ears looked back at him and turned around so that he could come back and stomp Henry Joe, but Henry Joe jumped up and ran for the fence as fast as he could.

Daddy Bob rode right in front of Ears popping his bullwhip. *Pow! Pow!* Ears turned to go after Daddy Bob and Tom, but Tom was too fast, and Ears could not catch them. By then Henry Joe had climbed over the fence.

Now the people in the stands were calling for Slim Windham. They knew that he was the best bull rider in east Texas, and they were sure that he could ride Ears.

Well, Slim got his bull rigging and climbed up on the chute. When Ears had been put back in the chute, Slim put the rigging on Ears, sat down on him, got his spurs ready, and just nodded his head. You have never heard so much yelling in your life as everyone cheered Slim on. Ears came out of the chute sideways. He landed on his back feet, stood like that for a second, and then jumped up in the air. Slim's shirttail came out of his pants and started popping like a whip. Ears came down on straight legs and jarred every bone in Slim's body. But Slim was a great rider, and he was still hanging on. Ears jumped in the air again, turned two times, and came down bellowing. Slim slid to the left, but he held on with his spurs. It looked like nothing could get him off Ears's back. All the people were standing up, yelling and throwing their cowboy hats in the air. Then everyone was suddenly quiet as Slim went flying over the fence. He landed in the grandstands right next to Nanny!

Well, no one else wanted to try to ride Ears. They loaded him up in Daddy Bob's trailer and took him back out to the ranch. As far as I know, he is still out there in the forest to this day. Maybe, if you go down by Elbow Marsh, you will see him out there eating grass with a few cows around. If you do, just be real quiet and leave him alone, because he is still the meanest bull in east Texas. Just ask Slim Windham!

Lep and the Wild Hog

Daddy Bob had a catch dog named Lep. A catch dog is a dog that catches an animal with his mouth and holds on until the cowboy can get there. Lep was the best catch dog that Daddy Bob ever had. He would have caught a bear if Daddy Bob had wanted him to. He was spotted like a leopard, and that was how he got his name.

Just before Christmas every year, Daddy Bob would go hunting for a wild hog for Christmas dinner. Now wild hog hunting is dangerous because wild hogs have two long tusks that stick out on each side of their mouths. If they catch you with one of those tusks, they can cut you open like a knife going through a feed sack. You have to be careful hunting hogs.

One year, just a few days before Christmas, Daddy Bob, Bubba, Danny Barrow, and his son Steve decided they would go hog hunting. They loaded the horses in their trailers, got the dogs, Rock, Brindle, Blue, and Lep, into the back of their pickup trucks, and drove down the forest road to the mayhaw thicket. They unloaded the horses, put their rifles on their saddles, and started off through the forest with the dogs running out in front. Sometimes, the dogs would get far ahead, but the cowboys carried cow horns, and by blowing them, they could call the dogs back.

They rode for about half an hour and did not see any hog tracks. The forest was getting very thick when, all of a sudden, they rode right up to a bunch of hogs. The hogs started running in every direction. Daddy Bob pulled his rifle out and started shooting. He shot one hog dead with his first shot. Some of the hogs ran over a small hill. Steve and Danny Barrow chased after them.

Bubba started chasing after a hog that he saw run into a thicket. He was running with Flag, and they had to jump over a log. When they came down on the other side, Flag tripped over some vines. Flag rolled completely over, and Bubba was thrown under a magnolia tree. When Bubba looked up to see if Flag was all right, he saw a big boar hog standing about ten feet away looking right at him. The hog had tusks that curled all the way back to his ears. Bubba looked around for his rifle, but he could not see it anywhere.

Bubba yelled, "Daddy Bob! Daddy Bob!" That was when the hog rushed him. Bubba grabbed a tree limb that was lying on the ground to fight the hog with, but just before the hog got to him, Bubba saw a spotted shape come streaking through the trees. It was Lep! Lep caught that hog right by the throat and knocked him clear around. Lep was hanging on to the hog as hard as he could, and he was not going to let go for anything. The hog pulled his head back and hit Lep with his tusks. Lep went rolling, but before the hog could turn back to Bubba, Lep hit him again. And that hog knocked Lep rolling again. The hog tried to turn back to Bubba, but Lep was right back on him. That hog knocked Lep all over the clearing, but Lep would not stop coming.

At last Daddy Bob heard the noise the two animals were making and came galloping through the trees. He pulled out his rifle, being very careful not to hit Lep, and he shot the hog dead. Daddy Bob was getting off Tom just as Danny and Steve Barrow came riding up. They all walked over to the dead hog and saw Lep lying beside it. Lep wasn't moving. Daddy Bob bent down to pet Lep and saw that he had been cut twelve times from his throat all the way down his legs. Bubba ran over to him crying, "No! Not Lep! He can't be dead!"

Danny Barrow took off his coat and wrapped Lep in it, saying, "We have to get him to the veterinarian." Daddy Bob got on Tom, and Danny handed Lep up to him. Then Daddy Bob and Bubba started galloping through the woods. They rode as fast as they could four of five miles to the road and another mile to the vet's house.

They took Lep in and laid him on the table in the vet's office. Daddy Bob and Bubba went outside to wait while the vet worked on Lep. As Daddy Bob walked back and forth, Bubba cried, "He's got to live; he can't be dead."

After about two hours, the vet came out and Daddy Bob asked, "How is he, Doc?"

The veterinarian said, "Well, I don't know if he will live or not. I sewed up his cuts, but there's not much more I can do for him. If he's still alive in the morning he'll have a good chance of making it."

Daddy Bob said, "Okay, I'll go back and get my pickup and come back for Lep."

Bubba wanted to stay with Lep. He went inside and saw Lep still lying there with a big bandage around his middle, his breathing pretty bad. Bubba petted him. Lep had saved his life. If Lep had not stopped the hog, it would have been Bubba lying in the hospital all cut up.

About an hour went by before Daddy Bob was back with the pickup. They took Lep out and put him in the back on some horse blankets and drove home. Daddy Bob carried him into the house and put him on the rug in front of the fireplace.

It was getting late, and Nanny said, "Bubba, it's time for you to go to bed."

"Please, Nanny," said Bubba. "I want to stay up and take care of Lep."

Nanny said, "You're tired and you need your sleep. There's nothing you can do for Lep. You go on to bed now."

Bubba lay in bed for a while, waiting for everyone to go to sleep, then he got up and went back to the living room. He sat up all night with Lep's head in his lap, wondering if Lep would still be alive in the morning.

Just before sunup, Lep opened his eyes and barked. Bubba woke up. He pushed Lep's water dish closer, and Lep drank it all. Bubba ran to Nanny and Daddy Bob's room yelling, "Nanny! Daddy Bob! Lep is better!"

As Nanny got out of bed she said, "What are you doing

up so early?"

Bubba shuffled his feet and looked at the ground as he told her how he had sat up with Lep all night.

Nanny said, "Boy, I ought to spank you!" But as Bubba looked up at her he saw she was smiling. "Well, let's go see how he is," she said.

In the living room Lep saw them and began wagging his tail. Nanny said, "Yes, I think he'll be all right."

Lep did live, and he got well, but he had been hurt pretty badly. Now he could never go into the woods hunting or helping with the cows because he could not keep up with the horses or the other dogs. His stomach hurt a lot, and he could not eat much. When Daddy Bob and Bubba had to ride into the forest to look for the cows, Nanny had to hold Lep back so that he would not try to follow them. Lep would sit there and howl—*Oww! Oww!*—because he could not run with the other dogs.

On a hot summer day a few months later, Daddy Bob and Bubba were sitting outside under the shade tree, and Lep was lying in the shade under the porch. Lep stood up and wandered into the woods. "I wonder where Lep is going," Bubba said.

Daddy Bob said, "Son, Lep is old and tired, and he hurts all the time. He's going into the woods to die in peace."

"But Daddy Bob, why would he go into the woods to die?" asked Bubba, as tears gathered in his eyes.

"He's a proud dog, Bubba. He was the best catch dog in

these forests, and he doesn't want anyone to see him when he is weak and dying," answered Daddy Bob.

They waited awhile, and then Daddy Bob said, "Okay, let's go see if we can find him." He got a shovel out of the barn while Bubba ran into the house to get something. They walked out to the trees together searching for Lep.

They finally found him lying on a pile of pine needles. Daddy Bob dug a hole and laid Lep there. Bubba reached into his pocket and took out two hog tusks and dropped them into the hole with Lep. Daddy Bob had saved them from the hog that had cut Lep up so badly.

As Daddy Bob covered Lep up with dirt, Bubba began to cry. Daddy Bob said, "Don't cry for Lep. He was a good dog and lived a good life. He's probably running through God's forest right now."

As they walked back to the house, Bubba was sure he heard Daddy Bob crying just a little.

Uncle Marshall and the Longhorn Bull

Uncle Marshall was Daddy Bob's uncle, and he had a small ranch about six miles through the woods from Daddy Bob's place. Uncle Marshall was sixty-five years old, and that was getting pretty old for doing cowboy work in the woods.

Uncle Marshall kept nearly a hundred cows, and he had a Longhorn bull out in the forest with them. Now, a Longhorn is as big and mean as a Brahma, and it takes a good cowboy to handle one. Uncle Marshall was getting too old to handle such a mean bull, and he decided to trade him to Bo Jordan for Bo's gentler Hereford bull.

Uncle Marshall knew that he would need some help, so he telephoned Daddy Bob and asked him to come over. Danny Barrow was at Daddy Bob's house shoeing some horses, and he said he would come too. They loaded the horses into the trailer and put the dogs, Brindle and Rock, in the back of the pickup. Bubba said he wanted to bring Flag too, but Daddy Bob said he did not want Bubba riding around when that Longhorn bull started fighting.

Danny, Daddy Bob, and Bubba all got into the pickup and drove over to Uncle Marshall's house. Uncle Marshall came out of the barn leading the paint horse that he had been riding for years and years. Daddy Bob looked at the horse and said, "Uncle Marshall, you shouldn't be out in the woods working wild cows with an old horse like that. He's too old and slow. You'll get yourself hurt one of these days. That horse must be twenty years old."

Uncle Marshall said, "Oh, he'll be all right."

Daddy Bob said, "Okay, but just remember, I warned you!"

They loaded Uncle Marshall's horse into the trailer and drove into the woods. Uncle Marshall said that the last time he had seen the Longhorn bull was in the pipeline clearing. Daddy Bob drove to the pipeline that ran through the forest owned by the pulp and paper company in Evadale.

They unloaded the dogs and horses, and Daddy Bob told Bubba to stay with the pickup. When they loaded the bull in the trailer, Bubba would shut the gate. Then Daddy Bob and Uncle Marshall started riding down the pipeline, and Danny Barrow rode toward Sid Mott's ranch in case the bull was over that way.

Soon Daddy Bob and Uncle Marshall heard the dogs barking. Then the bull came out into the pipeline clearing and stood there fighting the dogs. Brindle was trying to nip the bull on the heels to keep him moving while Rock was biting at his nose trying to turn him toward Daddy Bob.

Daddy Bob and Uncle Marshall got their ropes ready and ran their horses after the bull. The bull saw them and jumped toward the deep woods, but Daddy Bob threw his rope on him before he could reach the trees. The bull turned to fight Daddy Bob, but then Uncle Marshall's rope landed around his horns too. They both had him, one on each side. They kept their ropes tight so that the bull could not turn toward them and started leading him to the trailer.

They were almost to the pickup when that bull jumped straight up into the air, popped his head, and broke Daddy Bob's rope. When he came down, the bull smashed into the pickup, nearly turning it over, before Uncle Marshall could pull him away. Daddy Bob ran Tom to the trailer to get another rope.

Texas cowboys do "tie-down" roping. The rope is tied to the saddle horn, and the cowboy cannot drop the rope. Other cowboys do "dally" roping. They just wrap the end of the rope around the saddle horn and hold the rope tight with their hand, so that if the cow is too bad, they can drop the rope and run away. Texans use tie-down roping because cowboys are not supposed to run away. They think that if you cannot handle the bad cows, then maybe you should be something besides a cowboy. Maybe you should own a store and sell ice cream or something.

The bull charged at Uncle Marshall, but Uncle Marshall could not run away because his saddle was tied to the bull. All he could do was try to run in circles around the bull

while staying out of his way. Uncle Marshall's old paint horse was not fast enough to stay out of the way of the bull. The bull lunged and caught him, hitting the horse in the back and almost knocking him down. The horse tried to turn away from the bull, but the bull was too fast and hit

him in the side with his horns. Then the bull picked the horse up with Uncle Marshall still on him and threw them both on the ground. The dead horse landed on Uncle Marshall's leg. Uncle Marshall pulled and pulled, but he could not get his leg out from under the horse.

Bubba started honking the horn in the pickup, hoping that Danny Barrow would hear and come back.

The bull was standing right over the dead horse with his horns lowered to stick Uncle Marshall. Rock and Brindle were running in and biting the bull on the nose and legs trying to make the bull back away from Uncle Marshall. They kept the bull away until Daddy Bob's new rope came flying through the air and landed around the bull's horns. Tom reared back on the rope as hard as he could, pulling the bull's head around.

The bull turned and charged Tom and Daddy Bob. But Tom was a great cow horse and was watching every move the bull made. He saw that the bull was going to charge and raced out of the way. Rock and Brindle each jumped and caught the bull by the ears and hung on. Daddy Bob and the dogs fought that bull for ten minutes before Danny Barrow came galloping up and threw his rope on him. Then Danny and Daddy Bob pulled that bull into the trailer while Bubba ran over to see if Uncle Marshall was hurt.

When Daddy Bob and Danny had the bull in the trailer and had closed the gate, they rode over to Uncle Marshall, got down, and tried to push the dead horse off him. They could not do it, so Daddy Bob tied his rope around Uncle Marshall's saddle horn and Tom pulled the horse away.

They could see that Uncle Marshall had a broken leg. They loaded the dogs and horses into the trailer and then carried Uncle Marshall to the pickup and laid him in the back. Daddy Bob drove to the hospital in Vidor, and the doctor put a cast on Uncle Marshall's leg.

The next day, Daddy Bob, Bubba, and Nanny went to the hospital and picked up Uncle Marshall. When they got to his house, Uncle Marshall saw a young paint horse tied to the front porch. He asked Daddy Bob whose horse it was, and Daddy Bob said, "Uncle Marshall, I'm giving you this paint horse so that you'll have a good cowhorse to work with in the forest." Then they all went into the house, and Nanny made a big catfish supper.

The Hurricane Calf

You know that Daddy Bob had a bull named Ears, but he also had another bull named Hurricane. You see, Mauriceville was only a few miles from that part of the ocean called the Gulf of Mexico. Sometimes in the summer hurricanes would blow in from the Gulf and hit east Texas. A hurricane is a big storm with winds strong enough to blow houses away and with so much rain that the rivers overflow and flood the forests. When you hear that a hurricane is coming, all you can do is move your cows and horses deep into the forest on higher ground. Then you stay in the house hoping that the storm doesn't do too much damage.

Daddy Bob's house was built on the highest part of the ranch. Hurricanes would hit, and after they passed, the water in the bayous would overflow, and there would be a lake all the way around Daddy Bob's house. The water would be so high that cars and pickup trucks could not drive to the house. Cottonmouth water snakes would come up around the house and try to get out of the water. Sometimes alligators would be around the barn. It was a dangerous time.

When the water was so high, the only way to get out of the ranch was on the horses. Even then, the water would be up to Daddy Bob's knees. Nanny was a nurse, and she worked in the hospital in Vidor two days a week. She would have to ride a horse through the water with Daddy Bob to the farm road, where she parked the car. In the evening Daddy Bob would bring her horse out to the road, where Nanny would leave the car and ride home with him.

One summer day, Daddy Bob was listening to the radio while he and Bubba were branding calves. He heard the announcer say that there was a bad hurricane coming that would hit Port Arthur, Beaumont, Orange, and Lake Charles over in Louisiana. Mauriceville was only twenty miles from Beaumont and would be right in the path of the hurricane.

Daddy Bob said, "Come on, Bubba. We have to get everything ready for the storm." Daddy Bob had eight goats, and he told Bubba to take Flag and bring the goats to the barn. Then Daddy Bob got on Tom and rode off into the woods with Rock and Brindle. He had to move the cows deep into the woods where the wind would not be so bad.

While Bubba was rounding up the goats, Nanny was

getting the chickens, geese, turkeys, and guineas into the chicken house. Bubba came to help her after he had put all the goats into the barn. By then the wind was really starting to blow hard. They went around the barn and house putting away tools, buckets, saddle blankets, and anything else that might blow away.

Daddy Bob made sure that the cows and horses were safe in the forest. Then he rode to the fenced pasture that he kept for the cows that were going to have calves soon. As he rode around the pasture, he saw that one of the cows was missing. He saw her tracks and followed them to a hole in the fence. She had gone through the hole and into the forest. Daddy Bob rounded up the other cows and drove them into the barn.

When he was sure that the house, barn, and animals were ready for the hurricane, he went into the house. He saw Nanny and Bubba taking chairs from the porch into the house.

"Nanny," Daddy Bob said, "One of the cows that is going to have a calf got out of the pasture. I have to go look for her. You and Bubba stay in the house."

Nanny said, "You be careful. That hurricane is going to be here very soon."

Daddy Bob waved and turned Tom back toward the forest. He rode all through the woods looking for that cow. He had a long yellow raincoat on, and his hat was tied under his chin so that the wind would not blow it off.

Daddy Bob leaned forward over Tom, who hunched his back because the wind was so strong. It was dark now, and the rain was pounding down.

Finally, as Daddy Bob was crossing the dirt road that led to the Magnolia Refinery oil well, Tom stopped. Daddy Bob got down, turned on his flashlight, and saw the cow lying in the ditch that ran alongside the road. The ditch was full of water, with just the cow's head and side sticking out. The wind was howling through the trees, and the rain was beating down. Daddy Bob could hear tree limbs breaking off. He got down behind the cow and examined her. He saw that the calf was trying to come out, but its body was turned in the wrong position. If it did not get out soon, it would die. He got back on Tom and rode as fast as he could back to the house.

Nanny and Bubba were sitting by the fire when they heard Tom galloping into the yard. Daddy Bob came in and said, "Nanny, that cow is lying in a ditch full of water ready to have her calf, but the calf is twisted and can't get out. It's too late to save the cow. She's been lying in the water too long, but maybe we can still save the calf."

Nanny went to get a big flashlight out of the kitchen, then she and Bubba got their boots, raincoats, and hats on and went outside to get into the pickup. Daddy Bob rode Tom back to the ditch while Nanny drove the pickup behind him. Nanny and Bubba could hardly get their doors open to get out of the truck because the wind was blowing so hard.

Down the road, a big tree fell over and crashed to the ground.

They all got down into the ditch with the cow. Water was running over the tops of their boots. Daddy Bob and Bubba held the flashlights while Nanny looked at the cow. The top of the calf's head was trying to come out. Nanny said, "The calf can't come out and the cow is dying. We have to get the calf out now!" They knew they would not be able to save the cow, but if Nanny worked fast, maybe the calf would live.

Nanny had helped deliver a lot of babies at the hospital, but she had never helped deliver a calf. Daddy Bob grabbed the back legs of the cow and held them open while Nanny reached inside the cow and felt for the calf's legs. One front leg was bent the wrong way, and that was why the calf could not come out. Nanny grabbed the bent leg and began to slowly, slowly unbend it. Finally the leg was straight and pointed forward. Suddenly the calf's head and front feet were sticking out. "I did it!" Nanny said. "The calf can come now."

"But the cow is almost dead. We'd better pull it out," Daddy Bob yelled over the wind. "Bubba, go back to the truck and get the rope!"

"Yes, sir," Bubba yelled as he ran off through the rain. Bubba held the flashlight while Daddy Bob tied the rope around the calf's front feet. Slowly Daddy Bob and Nanny began to pull on the rope. For a few seconds they all thought the calf was stuck, but then, all at once, the calf slid out into the ditch. It was a little bull calf. Daddy Bob took the calf and put it on the front seat of the pickup. The cow was dead. Nanny drove the truck back home followed by Daddy Bob on Tom.

At home Daddy Bob carried the calf into the house and laid him on the rug in front of the fireplace. Then he went outside and put Tom in the barn. He rubbed Tom dry and gave him some hay and feed. Tom was so tired from fighting the storm that he could barely eat. Daddy Bob got a bucket and filled it with milk from the milk cow.

He went back into the house just as Nanny came out of the kitchen with a pot of hot water. She and Bubba took some old rags and started washing the calf. Daddy Bob heated the milk and put it into a big bottle with a nipple on it. He gave it to Bubba, and Bubba put the calf's head on his lap and fed him the milk. Then they sat around the fire and listened to the hurricane blowing around the house.

They kept the calf in the house all the next day. The hurricane had blown the roof off of Charles DeSadier's barn. Bubba and Nanny took care of the animals on the ranch while Daddy Bob went to help Charles with his roof.

Soon the calf was standing and getting stronger, so Nanny told Bubba that he had to take him out to the barn. Bubba fixed a very nice stall for the calf and filled it with straw. He and the calf got to be very good friends. He would feed it, brush it, and clean the stall every day. The calf would follow him around all day wherever he went. Nanny and Bubba decided to call him Hurricane.

One day a few months later, Daddy Bob came into the barn where Bubba was brushing Hurricane and told him about the county fair that was starting the next day in Orange. He said, "You could take Hurricane to the fair and show him in the calf contest. You might win a prize."

"What can I win?" asked Bubba.

"The boy or girl with the best calf will win a pair of new spurs," answered Daddy Bob.

So the next day they loaded Hurricane into the trailer and Daddy Bob, Nanny, and Bubba drove to Orange. They got out of the pickup and started walking through the fair-grounds leading Hurricane on a rope. Bubba could hardly believe his eyes. There were hundreds of people, so many rides, and food stands everywhere. Women brought their best quilts, jellies, and cakes to see who had made the best. There was horse racing, and that night there would be a rodeo. They passed a horseshoe-throwing contest and went through barns full of cows, goats, chickens, pigs, and horses.

Finally they came to a barn where the contest for the best calf was being held. Bubba took Hurricane into the arena with the other children and their calves. Daddy Bob and Nanny went to sit in the stands.

When the judge called a child's name, the child would lead his calf around the arena. The judge would see if the calf behaved well. Then the boy or girl would stop, and the judge would come to look at the calf up close to see if it had been well cared for. When the judge called Bubba's name, the boy led Hurricane around the arena. The judge told Bubba to stop and came over to him. He got down on his knees and felt Hurricane's legs. He stood up and said, "Thank you! You can take your calf away now."

Bubba led Hurricane over to the other calves and stood there waiting. The judge came over with three ribbons. He gave the white ribbon for third place to a little girl from Vidor who had a pretty black calf. Then he gave the red ribbon for second place to a boy from Orange. Finally he said, "The winner of the blue ribbon for best calf at the fair goes to Bubba and his calf, Hurricane." He hooked the ribbon to Hurricane's halter, and then out of a box he took a pair of spurs with little silver bells on them called jingle bobs. He gave them to Bubba, and Bubba shook his hand. Everyone in the barn clapped.

Bubba walked over to Nanny and Daddy Bob, and they all walked back to the trailer with Hurricane. After they had put Hurricane into the trailer, they went back to the fair, where they stayed the rest of the day. That night in bed, Bubba slept with his spurs in his hands and dreamed of all the rides he had been on and all the candy he had eaten.

A few weeks later, Daddy Bob told Bubba that it was time to let Hurricane go to the forest. Bubba was sad, but he knew Hurricane would be happy in the forest running with the other cows and bulls. They turned him loose down by Elbow Marsh, and Hurricane disappeared into the forest.

Hurricane became one of the best bulls that Daddy Bob ever had. Sometimes, when he was with the cows eating grass, he would hear the sound of the little bells on Bubba's spurs. He would stop munching on the grass, leave the cows, and look for the little boy that had taken such good care of him.

Toby Frederick's Three Goats

One time Daddy Bob and Bubba were over at Toby Frederick's house helping him with the branding. Bubba was keeping the irons hot while Daddy Bob was roping calves. When Daddy Bob caught a calf, he would bring it over to the fire and Toby would wrestle it to the ground and brand it. It was hot, dirty work, and at the end of the day both horses and cowboys were tired, hungry, and thirsty.

Toby told Daddy Bob and Bubba to come up to the house and have some iced tea before supper. As they were walking past the barn, Daddy Bob saw three young goats in a pen. He said, "Those sure are nice-looking goats you have, Toby."

Toby replied, "Yes, they're good ones, but I want to get rid of them. Me and my wife just have too many animals to take care of. I was thinking of taking them to the sale barn next Wednesday."

Daddy Bob stopped and looked at the goats for a few minutes, then turned to Toby and said, "I tell you what I'll do. I'll give you a roll of fence wire for them."

Toby said that a roll of wire would be a fair trade, and they walked on up to the house. They sat on the porch and drank glass after glass of iced tea. Daddy Bob and Bubba stayed for supper, and when they left, Daddy Bob said, "I'll bring that wire over tomorrow morning and pick up the goats."

The next day Daddy Bob and Bubba loaded the wire into the pickup and drove over to Toby's pulling the horse trailer. They unloaded the wire for Toby, loaded up the goats, and drove home. When they got there, they put the three goats in a small pasture behind the barn.

Bubba got up early the next day to go out and feed the goats. He went to the feed room and got a bucket of oats, then he walked to the pasture gate. There were no goats! He opened the gate, walked into the pasture, and saw where the fence wire had been torn loose from the fence post. Goat tracks led out through the hole in the fence toward the forest.

Bubba ran back to the house and into the kitchen where Daddy Bob was eating breakfast. "Daddy Bob! Daddy Bob! The goats got out of the pasture and went into the forest!"

Daddy Bob said, "Okay, we'll have to go catch them. Let's saddle the horses and go find them before something eats them." Nanny fixed them some sandwiches to take just in case it took all day.

Bubba and Daddy Bob rode out of the yard with Rock leading. It was a hot, hot day, with the sun beating down. The forest was shady, but it was still hot with no wind blowing through the trees. Soon swarms of mosquitoes were biting them, and big horseflies were on Tom's and

Flag's ears. They rode for an hour following the goat tracks. After a while they came to Cow Bayou and saw where two of the goats had turned off and the other had gone straight ahead.

Daddy Bob said, "Let's follow the two that turned off." He and Bubba got their ropes ready and followed Rock after the two goats. Soon they could hear Rock barking. When they found him, Rock had cornered the goats and was trying to keep them in one spot. The goats were jumping at Rock, but Rock was too fast for them and always got out of the way. When Daddy Bob and Bubba came riding up, the goats ran off in two different directions.

Daddy Bob said, "I'll go after the one that ran toward the cypress swamp, and you go after the other one, Bubba." He spurred Tom and rode off.

Bubba followed the goat and saw it run into a muddy piece of ground. He threw his rope and caught the goat around the horns. Flag tried to stop, but the ground was too muddy, and his feet started slipping. He slid to his knees, and Bubba went flying over his head. *Fwop!* Bubba landed in the mud on his face and stomach. He slid through the mud all the way to the goat. The goat was bucking on the end of the rope, trying to get away. Bubba tried to stand up, but the goat hit him in the seat of his pants with his head, and Bubba fell. *Fwop!* His face hit the mud again.

Flag was having trouble standing up again because his

feet kept slipping. Bubba tried to grab one of the goat's legs. The goat tried to run away, but because of the rope it could only run in a circle around Flag. Flag's legs got caught in the rope, and he fell over on his side in the mud. Finally Bubba caught one of the goat's horns and wrestled with it, but his feet slipped and he fell on his back in the mud, pulling the goat down on top of him.

All this time, Daddy Bob had been after the other goat. Tom chased the goat between two trees, but the trees were too close together, and Daddy Bob hit both of his knees against the trees, tearing a hole in his pants. My goodness, that hurt!

The goat had run into a blackberry thicket, so Daddy Bob and Tom went in after him. The thorns tore Daddy Bob's shirt and scratched his hands. The goat ran out of the thicket on the other side with Daddy Bob and Tom right behind him. They chased it through some more trees, and *whap!* Daddy Bob hit his head on a tree limb and almost fell off Tom. Daddy Bob's hat went flying away. Finally the goat ran into a clearing, and Daddy Bob threw his rope on him.

Daddy Bob rode back to where he had left Bubba, dragging the goat along behind him. Bubba was not there, but Daddy Bob could hear yelling through the trees. He rode toward the noise. When he came out of the trees, he saw a big moving lump of mud. "Now what in the world is that?" Daddy Bob wondered. He heard Bubba's voice coming from inside the mud. He rode closer and saw that the big lump of mud was really Flag, Bubba, and the goat, with a rope twisted all around them. Daddy Bob got off Tom, caught the goat, and helped Bubba get up. Together they got the rope loose from Flag's feet, and he stood up.

Bubba and Daddy Bob got on their horses and rode back along Cow Bayou to one of the small pens Daddy Bob had built in the woods to catch wild hogs. They put the goats in the pen and sat down under the tree to rest. Bubba was so covered with mud that he didn't look like a little boy any more. Daddy Bob had a big bump on his head, a torn shirt, torn pants, and scratched hands. He said, "Bubba, why don't you get those sandwiches that Nanny fixed for us?"

Bubba got up and went over to Flag. He had put the sandwiches into a pocket on Flag's saddle. He opened the pocket and took them out. They were mashed as flat as a piece of paper and covered with mud. Flag had fallen on them.

Daddy Bob said, "Well, we can't eat those. Come on, let's find that other goat."

They got back on their horses and rode along Cow Bayou with Rock following the tracks of the last goat. Soon Rock started barking and ran ahead. Daddy Bob and Bubba rode out of the trees and saw the goat standing on the bank of the bayou.

Daddy Bob said, "Let's get down off the horses. You come around after the goat on one side, and I'll come after it from the other. We have to catch it with our hands. The trees are too close together to rope it."

So they got down and walked toward the goat, one on each side of it. The goat looked first at Daddy Bob, then at Bubba, and jumped into the bayou. It was swimming as fast as it could for the other side.

Daddy Bob, like most cowboys, could not swim, so it looked as if the goat would get away. But then Bubba jumped into the water. That was dangerous, because there were cottonmouths and alligators near the bayou. Bubba was a good swimmer and he caught the goat around the neck when it was halfway across. He turned the goat around and began swimming back to the shore.

Just then, Daddy Bob saw the biggest alligator in Texas. This alligator's name was Moses, and he had been seen around Cow Bayou for years. Nobody had ever been able to catch him. He was fifteen feet long, and he was coming straight for Bubba and the goat.

Daddy Bob yelled, "Look out, Bubba! Moses is coming!" Then he picked up a big stick from the ground and threw it in the water where Bubba could get it. He turned around and ran to Tom to get his rifle off the saddle.

Bubba grabbed the stick that Daddy Bob had thrown to him and turned toward Moses. The goat could see Moses coming and was kicking in the water trying to get away. Bubba raised the stick over his head and hit Moses as hard as he could right between the eyes. Moses dived under the water. Bubba was turning in the water looking for Moses, but he could see nothing.

Now Daddy Bob was running down the bank with his rifle. He stopped at the water and saw Moses come up right behind Bubba. Bubba heard the water moving and turned around just in time to see Moses open his mouth. Bubba pushed the stick right into Moses's mouth. Moses closed his mouth with a snap and bit the stick in half.

Daddy Bob brought his rifle up and shot. *Blam!* He hit Moses in the nose. Moses started rolling over and over in the water. Daddy Bob shot again and knocked a piece out of Moses's tail. Moses dived under the water and swam away as fast as he could with Daddy Bob shooting at him all the way. *Blam! Blam! Blam! Blam!* Moses disappeared around a bend in the bayou.

Bubba pulled the goat to the bank. Daddy Bob tried to grab the horns, but he slipped, and all three of them fell back into the water. The goat tried to hook Daddy Bob with his horns and caught the front of Daddy Bob's shirt, tearing it completely off. Bubba was trying to catch the goat's back legs, but the goat kicked out and hit Bubba on his chin. Daddy Bob finally got his arm around the goat's neck and dragged him onto the shore. Bubba and Daddy Bob got the goat up the bank and used the rope to tie him to Tom. Then they got on their horses and took the goat back to the hog pen where they had taken the other two goats.

They drove the three goats back to the house with Rock

in front. When the goats were back in the pasture, Daddy Bob fixed the hole in the fence.

Nanny could not believe it when Daddy Bob and Bubba came into the house. Daddy Bob had no hat and no shirt, and there was a big hole in one knee of his pants. His hands were covered with scratches, and he had a big bump on his head. Bubba was soaking wet, covered with mud and mosquito bites, and had a big scratch on his chin.

"What in the world happened to you?" Nanny asked.

"Nothing," replied Daddy Bob.

Then, remembering the sandwiches that had been smashed during the attempts to round up the goats, together Daddy Bob and Bubba said, "I'm hungry!" Nanny fixed them more sandwiches while Bubba explained what had happened. After they had eaten, Daddy Bob and Bubba took baths and went straight to their beds, where they slept the rest of the day and all night.

The next morning, Bubba got up and went to feed the goats while Daddy Bob went to the kitchen for breakfast. Daddy Bob had just started eating when Bubba came running into the house yelling, "Daddy Bob! Daddy Bob! The goats got out of the fence again!"

Bubba and Snake

Danny Barrow lived on a small ranch. He was the horseshoer for the town and had cows and pigs in the woods just like Daddy Bob. He had a boy named Steve who was thirteen and a good cowboy. He also had two little girls. Johnny Ruth was seven, and Mary Lou was six.

One day Danny decided that he should get his girls a pony to ride around the ranch. He and Steve hooked the trailer to their pickup and drove to the sale barn in Kirbyville. They went inside and sat in seats close to the arena fence. They watched the horses come through first, but they did not see anything they wanted. Finally a shiny black pony came into the arena. He was wild-looking, and Danny Barrow was sure that the pony would not cost much. He listened to the bids and decided that they were low enough. It was a pretty pony, and Danny decided he wanted it.

Danny started bidding and finally got the pony for thirty dollars. He backed his trailer up to the loading chute and loaded the pony, and he and Steve drove home. There they took the pony out of the trailer and put him into a small pasture that was full of stinging weed but had a lot of good grass growing. Steve and Danny put the bridle and saddle on him, but he didn't like it at all and began to buck. He twisted and turned until he threw the saddle off. It took several more tries before they finally got the saddle on the pony.

Danny said, "I think we should call him Snake. The way he twists and turns when we try to saddle him reminds me of a snake. But we can't let Johnny Ruth or Mary Lou ride him yet. He's too wild." He led Snake to the front of the porch of the house and tied him there. In the house he phoned Daddy Bob.

"Hello, Daddy Bob? This is Danny. I bought a pony for my girls at the sale barn today, but it's really wild and needs training. Steve is too big to ride him, so I was wondering if Bubba would like to come over and help train him."

Daddy Bob said, "Wait a minute and I'll ask him." He called Bubba over to the phone and said, "Listen, Danny Barrow has a new pony that he wants you to help him tame for his girls to ride. Do you think you can do it?"

"Yes, sir," Bubba answered. "At least, I'd like to try."

Daddy Bob got back on the phone and said, "Okay,

Danny. We'll be over in a few minutes." He hung up the phone and went to tell Nanny while Bubba went to get the spurs that he had won at the county fair. Nanny wanted to come too, so they all got in the pickup and drove over to Danny's house.

When they got to Danny's ranch, they saw the pony tied to the porch and Danny's family standing in the front yard. "Thanks for coming! This is Snake," Danny said, motioning toward the pony. "Let's go on out to the pasture." He led Snake while they all walked into the stinging-weed field.

Danny held Snake still as Bubba started to climb up on him. Danny said, "Bubba, are you ready?" Bubba nodded his head yes and Danny handed him the reins. Before Bubba could climb on him, Snake reared up, and it looked as if he was going to hit Danny with his front feet. Danny jumped back but tripped and fell in the stinging weed. Ow! He got up as fast as he could and started scratching and scratching. "Ow! Ooh! Ouch!" he yelled. Everyone was laughing.

Danny grabbed Snake's reins and held him still while Bubba tried again to climb on him. Again Danny said, "Bubba, are you ready?" Bubba nodded yes, and took the reins from Danny. This time he got on the pony. The pony took off, bucking as hard as he could straight down the pasture, then he turned around and bucked all the way back. Bubba didn't have any trouble hanging on. It was as easy as riding a rocking horse. But then Snake started

jumping straight up and coming down stiff-legged, trying to jar Bubba off. Everyone was yelling, "Hang on, Bubba, hang on!"

Finally Snake saw that he could not buck Bubba off. He took off running as fast as he could, straight for a tree that was growing in the middle of the pasture. Nanny yelled, "Look out, Bubba!" Bubba saw what Nanny meant. The tree had a low limb, and Bubba knew what Snake was going to do. That pony was going to run under the tree limb and try to knock Bubba out of the saddle. Bubba ducked, and the tree limb passed over him. If Snake had started bucking then, he would have thrown Bubba for sure, but Snake just kept running.

Bubba straightened up in the saddle and saw the horse heading for a barbed-wire fence. Everyone knew that Bubba was in real trouble now. Either Snake was going to run right up to the fence and stop so fast that Bubba would go flying over the fence, or he was going to turn real fast right at the fence so that Bubba would fall off into the barbed wire.

Bubba could see they were getting close to the fence, and he held on for dear life. But then Snake fooled everyone. Instead of stopping or turning, Snake jumped clear over the fence like a deer. His back feet caught the top string of the wire and snapped it in two. *Ping!* The wire shot through the air. Snake landed in the front yard and started bucking again.

Everyone was yelling, "Ride him, Bubba, ride him!" Snake bucked out of the yard and onto the road. Everyone followed after them. Uncle Marshall was driving along when he saw Snake and Bubba come bucking down the road followed by Daddy Bob, Steve, Danny, Nanny, Johnny Ruth, Mary Lou, Mrs. Barrow, and Danny's dog, Blackie. Snake bucked right by Uncle Marshall's pickup. As they went by, Snake kicked out and smashed one of Uncle Marshall's headlights.

Ida and Wanda Spurlock, two elderly sisters, had a house just down the road from Danny Barrow's place. On this day, Ida was outside on the porch in her rocking chair when she heard a big commotion just down the road. Wanda was in the kitchen. Ida yelled, "Wanda! Come out here and look at this! I've never seen anything like it!" Wanda came running out onto the porch to see what was going on. They saw a black pony with a little boy on it bucking toward their house, and running behind them were Daddy Bob, Steve, Danny, Nanny, Johnny Ruth, Mary Lou, Mrs. Barrow, and a dog. Behind them all was Uncle Marshall in a pickup with a smashed headlight.

The two sisters could scarcely believe it when Snake bucked right up into their yard. He bucked around the side of the house. Ida and Wanda ran through the house and out onto the back porch. They saw Snake and Bubba come around the corner into the back yard. Snake crashed right through the gate of the chicken yard, and still Bubba hung on. Chickens started squawking and flapping their wings, trying to get out of the way. Snake knocked over the chicken feed and kicked the water bucket over. He ran right over a turkey, and feathers went flying everywhere.

Snake bucked through the wooden chicken-yard fence and into the vegetable garden, and Bubba was still hanging on. They went through the string beans, bean poles falling over behind them and wrapping around Bubba's legs, through the tomatoes, tomatoes flying through the air like baseballs, and into the watermelons. You could hear the melons burst every time Snake hit the ground. *Splat! Splat! Splat!*

As he came out of the garden, Snake ran under the clothes line. The line wrapped around Bubba, and the clothes were dragging along in the dirt with the bean poles. A sheet fell over Bubba's head and he could not see a thing. He could tell when Snake crashed through the wall of the pigpen by the smell. Pigs took off in every direction.

Finally Snake had had enough. He stood there breathing hard, just too tired to buck anymore. Sweat was rolling down his sides, and his head was hanging down. Bubba got the sheet off his head. He was so sore and tired, he could hardly move, but he had outlasted Snake. Everyone ran up to him, and Daddy Bob said, "Boy, you sure rode that horse, didn't you?"

Ida and Wanda came running down off the porch yelling, "Danny Barrow, just look at what your pony has done to our garden. Who is going to fix all this mess, and what about our tomatoes and watermelons? Who is going to catch all those chickens and pigs and mend those fences?"

"Don't worry," Danny said. "We'll catch the chickens and pigs for you right now, and tomorrow I'll come over and fix the fence and the pigpen. When they're ready to be picked, I'll bring you tomatoes and watermelon from our garden."

After they had gotten the chickens back into the chicken yard and the pigs back in the pigpen, they all went back to Danny's house. Bubba rode Snake, and Snake behaved like a good pony. They left Snake tied to the porch and went into the house to have a big supper. All through the meal, everyone talked about the great ride that Bubba had made.

When it was time to go home, Bubba got back on Snake and started riding him toward the barn while Danny went to get a bucket of oats. Bubba was riding by the back porch thinking what a good pony Snake was now when Snake dipped his head and made a big jump. Bubba was thrown backward. He hit the porch screen, slid down the wall, and hit the ground. When he came down, Snake stepped on Bubba's arm, leaving a big scratch.

Danny heard the noise and ran to see what had happened just as Snake ran past. Snake kicked out and hit Danny in the stomach, right on his belt buckle, and knocked him head first into the oat barrel. Daddy Bob grabbed Snake's reins and stopped him. He put Snake in the barn and ran back to see how Bubba was. Everyone was there trying to help him up. "You're lucky it's only a scratch," said Nanny. "He could have broken your arm."

Mrs. Barrow looked around and said, "Where's Danny?"

"I think he went to the feed room," answered Steve.

They all walked over to the feed room. They could hear, "Mmph! Mmph!" As they went in, they saw the oat barrel with Danny's legs sticking out, kicking in the air. Daddy Bob and Steve pulled him out as everyone laughed.

"That is one mean pony," said Danny. "I think Bubba will have to ride him every day for awhile."

For the next few weeks, Bubba went over to Danny's house and rode Snake. Finally Snake was ready for Mary Lou and Johnny Ruth to ride. He turned out to be a real good pony, even as good as Flag. Well, almost.

Daddy Bob and Moses, the Alligator

It was October, but the weather was still very hot.
Daddy Bob, Nanny, and Bubba were sitting out on the front
porch in their rocking chairs with the full moon shining
down on the forest. It was Friday night, and Bubba asked,
"What are we going to do this weekend?"

Nanny said, "I sure would like to have a big fish supper
tomorrow night. We could ask Danny Barrow and his family to come over to eat with us, but we're out of fish. You
and Daddy Bob will have to go fishing."

Daddy Bob said, "We could go fishing tonight. You want
to run a trotline through the swamp, Bubba?"

Bubba loved to go trotline fishing because they could
camp out in the forest all night. "Sure, Daddy Bob."

Nanny got up and said, "I'll go fix you some food to cook
for breakfast."

Daddy Bob and Bubba went out to the barn and saddled Tom and Flag. Then they went back into the house and filled a pack with head lamps, a frying pan, plates, cups, a lantern, a trotline, fish bait, and some bacon and eggs that Nanny gave them for breakfast. They took the pack and two sleeping bags outside and tied them on the horses. Nanny came out onto the porch and kissed them both good night. They rode out of the yard with Rock running beside the horses.

They had to ride about three miles through the forest to the edge of the swamp. Daddy Bob always kept a rowboat tied to a big cypress tree. They tied the horses to a tree and took the saddles off. Bubba gathered some wood for a fire while Daddy Bob laid out the sleeping bags. Soon the fire was going, and Daddy Bob lit the lantern and hung it on a tree limb.

They went down to the boat and put their head lamps on their cowboy hats. With the trotline and the fish bait, they got into the boat and started rowing through the cypress trees. They found a good place, and Daddy Bob started fixing the trotline.

A trotline is a long, thick string with fishhooks every few inches. Daddy Bob tied one end of the line to a tree stump, and then they rowed to a fallen tree, and he tied the other end to it. Bubba rowed slowly back along the line while Daddy Bob put bait on all the hooks. When they were finished, they rowed back to their camp.

They pulled the boat up out of the water and got into their sleeping bags. Rock had run into the forest, but he came back and laid by the fire. Daddy Bob and Bubba lay there looking up at the stars through the trees and talking. But soon the horses, Rock, the man, and the boy were deep asleep.

About two hours later, Daddy Bob got up and woke Bubba too. Then he put some more sticks on the fire while Bubba got his boots on. When Bubba was ready, they got into the boat and rowed out to the trotline. They had caught four catfish, two perch, a bass, and a buffalo fish. Daddy Bob put new bait on the hooks, and they went back to the camp. They put the fish into a fish trap and left them hanging in the water. When they were finished, they got back into their sleeping bags and went back to sleep.

Not long after that, Daddy Bob woke up. Rock was barking and looking out toward where the trotline was tied. Bubba sat up and asked, "What is Rock barking at?"

"I don't know," Daddy Bob said. "But we better go check the trotline again."

They put on their boots, turned on the head lamps, and walked over to the boat. Daddy Bob pushed it into the water and they got in. They rowed over to the trotline and started pulling it up. My goodness! They had caught some fish, but something had eaten them right off the line.

Daddy Bob leaned over the side of the boat to pull up more of the line when there was a big bump against the boat. He tried to grab the side, but his fingers slipped, and he fell into the water with an enormous splash. Daddy Bob's hat came off and sank under the water with the head lamp still on it.

Bubba looked around for Daddy Bob, and his light shone right into the eyes of Moses, the alligator. Then he saw Daddy Bob stand up in the waist-deep water. Moses was going straight for Daddy Bob! Bubba yelled, "Look out, Daddy Bob! Moses is right behind you!"

Daddy Bob turned around and pulled out his big Bowie knife just as Moses got to him. Daddy Bob jumped out of the way at the last second, and as Moses shot by, Daddy Bob jumped on his back. Moses rolled over, and they both went under the water.

Bubba called, "Daddy Bob! Daddy Bob!" It looked like the water was boiling where Daddy Bob and Moses had gone under. The water was splashing everywhere. But all of a sudden, the water was still. Bubba looked all around and listened as hard as he could. Nothing! It was completely quiet. Not even a frog was croaking. Then, far away, Bubba saw the water splash up in the middle of some cypress trees. He heard splashing, yelling, and the roar of an alligator. Daddy Bob was standing up in the water holding his knife high above his head. He came down with the knife just as Moses hit him and knocked him down into the water. They both disappeared under the water again.

Bubba rowed the boat over to where they had gone under, but he couldn't see or hear anything. Then, far off, he heard more yelling and fighting. He looked around but he still couldn't see anything. Bubba called, but there was no answer. He rowed around all through the trees calling over and over for Daddy Bob, but he never heard a thing.

Finally he decided he had better go back to the camp before he got lost. Maybe Daddy Bob had gotten away from Moses and was back at the camp. He rowed back to the shore, but Daddy Bob was not there. Bubba was scared, and he didn't know what to do.

Bubba sat there by the fire. Sometimes he would stand up and call, "Daddy Bob! Daddy Bob!" But there was never any answer. Finally he decided he had better go home and get Nanny. He saddled Flag, got on him, and rode home as fast as he could.

It was about four o'clock in the morning when he got to the house. He got off Flag and ran into the house into Nanny's bedroom.

"Nanny! Nanny! You have to get up! Daddy Bob fell out of the boat, and he's fighting Moses down in the swamp. I can't find him." Bubba began to cry.

Nanny got up and gave him a big hug. She said, "Don't cry, Bubba! We'll find him." Then Nanny put on a dress and a shirt on over it. On the way out, she put on some rubber boots and a hat and grabbed a head lamp and Daddy Bob's rifle. Nanny and Bubba got into the pickup and drove down to the swamp. They could not see or hear anything of Daddy Bob and Moses.

Nanny said, "Bubba, you stay here and keep the fire going so Daddy Bob can find us if he gets away from Moses. I'm going to take the boat and go look for him." She put on the head lamp and took the rifle and climbed into the boat. Bubba gave the boat a push, and Nanny paddled away into the darkness. Then he went back to the fire and added more sticks until the fire was big enough to be seen for a long way.

Bubba sat down, and Rock came over and laid his head in Bubba's lap. "Rock, I wonder if we'll ever see Daddy Bob again," Bubba said. Rock whimpered.

Nanny rowed through some huge old cypress trees with long strands of moss hanging down. She sat there listening to the night. She thought she heard something off to her left and began to row that way. Yes! She did hear something! She rowed faster, and as she looked around, the light of her head lamp fell on Daddy Bob. He was leaning against the trunk of a tree with water up to his waist. His shirt was gone except for the sleeve of his right arm. He was scratched and cut all over, but he still held the big Bowie knife in his hand.

"Stay away, Nanny," Daddy Bob yelled. "That 'gator is still around here somewhere."

Just then Moses came out of the water and leapt for Daddy Bob. Both of them went down under the water.

Nanny grabbed the rifle. She could see Daddy Bob and Moses wrestling in the water, but she was afraid she would hit Daddy Bob if she fired. Moses came up for air, and Nanny hit him in the head as hard as she could with the paddle two or three times.

Well, that was enough for Moses! This cowboy he had in the water was the toughest thing he had ever fought, and now someone was hitting him in the head! He had been cut several times by the Bowie knife, and he was sore and tired all over. He was going home! He swam away as fast as he could, but when Nanny started shooting at him, he swam even faster.

Daddy Bob staggered over to the boat, and Nanny helped him in. Nanny could see how tired and hurt he looked. One leg of his pants was torn off, and both of his cowboy boots were gone. He fell asleep, and Nanny rowed back to the shore.

Nanny and Bubba helped Daddy Bob out of the boat and laid him into the back of the truck. Bubba tied Tom to the truck, and then he and Rock sat in the back with Daddy Bob as Nanny drove slowly home.

At the house, Nanny put bandages on Daddy Bob's cuts and made a big breakfast. Daddy Bob ate and ate, then he fell into bed, where he slept all day. I don't know where Moses went, but I am sure that he slept all day, too.